TRAVELING ON

TRAVELING ON
Fifty Years of Poetry and Sculpture

Michael Robbins

International Psychoanalytic Books (IPBooks)
New York • http://www.IPBooks.net

Traveling On: 50 Years of Poetry and Sculpture
Published by IPBooks, Queens, NY
Online at: www.IPBooks.net

Karen Sheingold provided the photos of the sculptures

ISBN: 978-1-956864-46-5

Photo of sculpture *Looking Backward* made more than 50 years ago during my personal psychoanalysis which was part of training to become a psychoanalyst

Dedicated to those who have journeyed with me,
especially those who have stayed on the bus.

CONTENTS

INTRODUCTION

It was a little more than 50 years ago that I began to write poetry and do wood sculpting. I have written poetry in what in retrospect appear to be three stages. My first awkward efforts, beginning in my early 40s, were probably expressions of unrest in my marriage that eventually ended in divorce. I include them for historical interest because I don't think they are very good. The next series were efforts to commemorate important occasions in the lives of persons I cared about, all sadly now deceased. My inner urge to write poetry developed subsequently and slowly. I call it an urge rather than a muse as it came from the periodic need to express a feeling state rather than from a drive to write poetry or from an external event. This last series for the most part represents efforts to confront aging, infirmity, and my eventual passing. Except for "Eternity," made from the stump that remained of the fallen birch that inspired the poem "Twin Birches," my sculptures were not made in response to specific events. I have tried to match the photographs

to the events with which the moods or feelings
I recall at the time I made each sculpture most
closely resonate.

First period: 1970-1980

(dates are approximate)

Contingencies (Hedging Bets)

Would you be my true love
if things changed and when?
Would-Be Valentines are spared
the pains of mortal men.

In fantasy our souls embrace.
In lands beyond my carapace
while what is here, within my skin
remains inviolate, and chaste.

Oh, will you be my Valentine?
It's not secure, you know.
That land between the hearth
and outside in the snow.

Arrhythmia (My Symbiotic Valentine)

Will you be my heart, Dear Heart?
But only understand.
The rhythm once you are inside
must match my marching band.

If I should wish to sleep at night
you cannot toss about,
else I must buy a pacemaker
and selfishly cut you out!

Chess Game, mahogany

Poems in the next series were written for neighbors I admired in commemoration of their special occasions, and for my best friend on his 40th, all, sadly, now deceased.

For the 25th Anniversary of the Solomons Around 1980.

("The Institute" refers to the Boston Psychoanalytic Institute where Len Solomon and I had done our psychoanalytic training together, including having the same analyst.)

I vowed to write an epic work to mark the great event.
One possessed of wide appeal like war and peace, detente.
I'd biograph the Solomons, find recipe for success.
Reveal it to an eager world waiting rescue from distress.

I interviewed the happy pair
keenly anticipating
sensationalism, tips, and special ploys
that won them silver plating.

Some violence or kinky sex?
I asked, expectantly.
They answered, "Just respect and love."
I sighed dejectedly.

Perhaps you've shared some special crimes
our viewers might wish to see?
Alas, but all they could report
was plain stability.

I failed with yet another theme,
that of technology.
No pills or databanks were used
to maintain their harmony.

Well, how about survival, then?
A marriage theme like "Jaws."
"You mean the Institute?" said Len.
That marriage fraught with flaws!

I finally gave up in defeat.
Their values wouldn't sell.
Fidelity is an outmoded state
where voyeurs don't wish to dwell.

So, failing in my epic quest
I have but this to say:
Give me twenty-five more years to think.
Perhaps I'll find a way!

Birthday Celebration for Neighbor Deborah Hauser Around 1975

Why are we gathered here, good folk?
Another of those awful things
like Legionnaires having a disease
or bribery of kings?

You know they shoot our national bird?
Our country's no longer first.
Our Presidents are impeachable.
Even this is not the worst.

I've heard our idols may also change.
Our fairy-tale Queens.
Our sources of stability.
Just imagine what that means?

Esther Williams selling swimming pools.
Our mermaid of the sea?
Kate Smith, God Bless America,
in professional hockey?

There's one such rumor recently,
I hope it isn't true,
were pinups lacking Grable's legs
I don't know what I'd do.

So, Debbie, You must never change.
I need mythology.
Let's drink tonight to something else
and keep my sanity.

Seated Woman, red cedar

Intoxication

(For Larry Strasburger's 40th Birthday party 6/28/1975 to accompany gift of a nitrous oxide cylinder (laughing gas) which we shared)

Inflate this life's balloon.
Breath deep its sweet bouquet.
On Jove's own sweet perfume
with friends we'll drift away.

The blossom's time soon done
it vanishes like the rain.
That chance not grasped is gone
makes sweeter what we retain.

Breathe deep the snuff of life
and laugh away the years.
Time cuts us like a knife.
Anesthetize our tears.

Self-loss transmutes to pleasure's gain.
Let's banish reality.
In floating we untether pain.
Fleeting moments to be free.

Oh, still our nagging doubts
for these brief hours, at least.
Stone reason's cautious shouts.
Let's celebrate this feast!

Joy, red cedar

Poems written since 2005

This final group represents my efforts to come to terms with life's changes, especially those that mark aging, infirmity and eventually dying. They express emotional states that seemed to obsess me.

Loon Seasons

I watched you glide across the lake.
No urgent frantic winged flight.
And as I tracked your serene wake
abruptly you were gone from sight.

Breathless I sat so long, and then
elsewhere you appeared again.
To trust takes time but now I ken.
Loon seasons come – but where and when?

Surface and depth of life you know.
And back and forth betwixt you go.
What is that other world you see
when I'm not with you nor you with me?

The seasons pass yet I come back
in vigil watching for your track.
But still, I wonder where you go
when I cannot see you so?

Perhaps it's I who loses sight?
I who wanders into night.
Where is that place to which we go?
And will again we see the light?

The sun sets crimson o'er the lake.
The freezing ice shows no loon wake.
Summer glides too quickly past.
Shall somewhere else we meet at last?

Twin Birches

You grew together.
The white and the gray.
Twin birches
guarding the house.
Under your sheltering branches
intertwining your lives with ours.
Overlooking lake, mountain
and lives within.

Winds blew.
Storms came and went.
Ice, snow and rain.
Life's seasons passed.

Through times when lightning struck
your limbs cracked and fell
yet resolute you stood.
Watching, sheltering, timeless.

Leaves budded, grew, turned orange and
fell.
Renewed as the seasons came and went.
The family grew too,
through splits, hurts and healings.
Yet still we were together.

I guess it had to end.
Weary from sheltering all of us
from the relentless buffeting of life.
A macro-burst they called it.
And the white birch fell.

Today they came
to cut you down.
Chip and scatter your ashes
on the slope of eternity.

You left the grey to stand alone
and me no shelter from life's storms.
Without embracing limbs and shading leaves
we'll be next to go
to reunite with you again
in the grasp of eternity.

**I saved the stump of the white birch and
sculpted from it the two conjoined figures.**

"Eternity" is the name I gave to this sculpture completed in 2004
from the fallen birch about which this poem was taken

A Skim of Ice

A skim of ice is on the pond.
A sign that winter's coming on.
Though chill I feel upon my skin
I know that spring will come again.

Summer seemed to have no end.
Meadows to mow and outdoor fun.
Bountiful harvest round the bend
and roads that shimmered in the sun.

When winter came in youth I learned
that summer faithfully returned.
Near the fire spent time till spring,
warming myself 'neath folded wing.

But now I am not quite so sure.
Things end but do they then return?
Life's changes I may not endure.
I won't forever live and learn.

Some say that humans resurrect.
The stone rolls back that souls protect.
While life writ large renews it's true,
we single seeds but once are new.

False comfort offered to the self.
The one I came to be from naught
now senses the chill that's coming on
as in life's cycle I am caught.

Some year the spring will come again.
Though meadows will surround with bloom,
in winter's thrall will I remain.
No thaw will come to give me room.

Poems of aging written in my late 70s
Summer 2012

Epitaphy

Feels like a graveyard when I awake.
The family of my dream
vanished and I am here alone.
The pillow beside me unruffled.

I walk through empty rooms
whose furnishings sit silently.
Filled with all life's memories.
Waiting for owners to return
and animate them again.

Memories rise up to haunt me.
Their ghostly presences beckon,
enticing me to rejoin them
and sear me again with pain of loss.

At the door of her room my thoughts call
out
Get up sleepy head, you slept the whole
night through;
Good morning, good morning to you.

Sometimes I can hear her voice respond.
For an instant fooling my wishful mind.
But then I can't but understand,
it's just the echo of my thoughts.

I see her dolls, his star charts, ball and
glove.
Out the window their bikes and skis,
the tree house where they played.
Where are they now but in my heart?

I sit upon the porch, look out and wait.
Soon I will be gone too.
And the rooms empty even of memory.

Grief, cherry

The Paradox of Seasons

Fall is coming again.
Time moves on.
Life moves on.
But the clocks fall back
as if to slow fate down.
They give us the illusion of
another hour to sleep.
But can they halt the cold?

Traffic Patterns

You had the nerve to cut me off!
Weaving in and out.
Roaring ahead then slamming on the brakes.
Where are you going in such a hurry?

A poet now dead told us
the paths of glory lead but to the grave.
Perhaps you have another destination
In mind?

And now, once in the lead
you meander along.
The solid line restraining
when I want to pass and move ahead.

When a space before me opens
you speed up going nowhere fast.
A crazy world indeed.
But do I know where I am going?

Unthinkable

The Dalai Lama is 77!
So the newspapers say.
He nears the time to go to heaven.
Or wherever Buddhists stay.

I am senior to a God!
Yet he should lead the way.
If ever there were a thing seemed odd
I wait for him to say.

He will come back it's said.
But can I wait to see?
It's likely he will soon be dead
and what will happen to me?

We'll reach that unremembered state
but he'll start over again.
Who knows what will be my fate?
What end I will begin?

Roots

It's harder to arise.
I drift into a daze.
Where's all that purpose I did prize?
The trails I once did blaze?

They say it's good to grow some roots.
But rooted to the spot?
My feet like lead within my boots.
I hope that I won't rot.

I Never Had Time to Write a Poem

Who had time to write a poem?
More important stuff to do.
I had to work and make a home
and see big projects through.

Now life's chores are mostly done.
The projects are complete.
No further deadlines there to meet.
Just time to have some fun.

But time hangs heavy like a shroud.
The days fly by like birds.
My actions no longer speak so loud.
Now what about some words?

Wearing Old Clothes in Maine

Here by the lake it's summer.
A time to have some fun.
I'm dressed in old worn clothes.
My life's work's mostly done.

Does summer change with time?
The clothes that I wore then
seem for a different clime.
Another race of men.

Each piece had its occasion.
Memories now flood back.
Filled with emotional persuasion
this summer seems to lack.

What's to dress for now?
My clothes worn near to rag.
To unclothed fate I bow.
So put things in a bag.

Can I really hope to find
in this unfamiliar nation
a haven that seems kind;
an Army of Salvation?

The Fall

Yesterday I slipped and fell.
It's happened countless times before.
Not a thing on which to dwell.
Get up, dust off, go back for more.

My child's knees scrubbed raw by ground.
I'd spring up and folks would say
There's nothing can keep him down!
Arise and seize another day.

I've left that child self behind.
Hard knocks my journey couldn't stay.
I ran the course ahead to find
new peaks to conquer on the way.

Life has falls and sometimes breaks.
Choices to make with roads to take.
Some are good and some mistake.
Get up, dust off and shed the ache.

The fall they say has great portent.
When summer's leaves come wafting down.
Though heralding winter's cruel intent
we know that spring will smooth its frown.

Life holds for us yet greater falls.
The fall from grace from heedless acts.
The hurts from which we build the walls
that from the love we want distract.

So now there's yet another slip.
Hardly worth noting it might seem.
No blow or hurt to make me trip.
No misstep taken in a dream.

The truth you see, that casts its pall,
is that I must be getting old.
That's all it took to make me fall.
Can I yet rise again and hold?

Blindness

(Subsequent to a fateful ophthalmological
appointment end of 2014)

He sat there before me,
his manner well suited
to make the announcement.
The doomsday pronouncement
that could not be refuted.

He said, "for your own good
I now find
that you are blind."

Our chart is before you.
To its letters you are blind.
We have little choice
but to treat you in kind.

No metaphor this.
No game peek-a-boo.
My license was taken.
I was banished from view.

He must be mistaken!
Because I am blind
to the reality they see
I'm cast adrift in a world
that cannot see me.

My right is their wrong.
I no longer belong.

Can we see one another?
Oh, why do we not?
These questions of life
obsess me a lot.

A doctor of mind's eye,
my mission to free
and bring insight to those
blind to selves and to me.

That blindness is named.
Transference we call it.
With words it is framed.
Vision's path can be lit.

I've been told I am blind,
my license rescinded.
A self was erased.
An identity effaced.

If I'm judged to be blind by you
And I know you are blind to me,
then my doomed soul eternally wanders
waiting endless for someone to see.

The Track Left Behind

(The single track behind my property shared
by an infrequently running freight train
and Amtrak was abandoned by Amtrak when
it moved its trains to a route a few miles
away.)

The tracks have been abandoned
that run next to my place.
The railway is deserted.
Of the train there is no trace.

Their rhythm was my clock.
Back and forth each day they went.
For my soul an anchor rock.
A refuge when confused and spent.

The diesel dragons lit the night.
Their beacon watching o'r the deep.
Until the coming of the light
my guardians as I did sleep.

Now I watch the tracks and wait
for ghosts of memory to come back.
The warn of distant whistle blowing.
Apparition roaring down the track.

But the route's no longer taken.
The station's tumbled down.
My senses are sore mistaken
and my hopes again are blown.

I see the ties are broken.
Weeds are growing in each crack.
Remembered words no longer spoken.
There is no going back.

Then people came and went,
with future lives now past.
Their destinies new now spent.
Their life journeys done at last.

I'm told they moved the line.
Of the trains there is no trace.
Just memories for me to pine
in this now forsaken place.

In my vigil I recall
the broken ties of life.
The ghostly shards of fall
The pain from times of strife.

In childhood other dragons led.
Some to great adventure.
But others to states of fear and dread
in places I wished I had not tread.

MICHAEL ROBBINS

Belching smoke their whistles blew
in Dopplerized crescendo.
Another journey by us flew
leaving memory's diminuendo.

In dream I reconstruct the trail
and through my mind's eye hear
once again that whistle wail
as memories, lost, appear.

Where are those places I did stay.
The life that I once led.
Those stations along the way.
My buddies now long dead?

The Bluefish are Running

(Memorial for Larry Strasburger
(July 2, 1935 – January 3, 2015))

Get up!
The bluefish are running.
The day is bright with promise.
Come join the chase.

But yet you linger.
You tarry in another place
where time no longer matters
and eternity fills the space.

Once your voice sang out "let's go,
come and join the chase."
Excited by your passion
our steps followed in your pace.

Do you dream of bluefish still
while life for us moves on?
Or is it we who dream of you
and the void we cannot fill.

When fishers vacate life's brief space,
fleeting ripples on time's vast sea,
who will give chase when bluefish run
throughout eternity?

Dysfunctional Family
(With Apologies to Mother Goose)

(Written prior to amputation of my second
toe because of bunions and hammertoe
January 2015)

I am an old man
and I live in my shoe.
I've got five fractious children.
You may think you know the rest
but I doubt that you do.

Five of us crowd ourselves into this place.
Truly there's not enough usable space.
Eenie keeps hammering at Meenie,
believing he keeps him from Mynie.
And Meenie is bent out of shape
forcing Eenie to stay in his place.
Our home is dysfunctional and abrasive.
Of this truth we cannot be evasive.

Oh Dears won't you please understand?
Please heed my parental command.
Eenie and Meenie stop fighting.
Our welfare as family you're blighting.

TRAVELING ON

While the other four children
have grown straight and tall,
Meeni is bent out of shape
and abrading us all.
Your brethren act fine
but you won't toe the line.

I've given you therapy help
in hopes it will straighten you out.
Though my effort is truly heartfelt
you stubbornly continue to pout.

There's not enough room in our shoe
to fit us and the rowdiness of you.
You're coming between Eenie and Mynie.
So Meenie you've just got to go.

Myself, Eenie, Mynie and Moe
we will each of us henceforth be blue.
But if our family is to grow
what else dear Meenie can we do?

Going, Going, Gone!

When young I pushed on ahead.
Climbing mountains of self-doubt.
I ran fast to escape from my dread
of a self I knew little about.

My teachers said "walk, do not run!"
Senseless rules that I had to conform.
There was neither room for fun
nor for my rebellious storm.

At night when freed up to dream,
Super or Bat I might seem.
"Up, up and away" toward the sun.
In fantasy life was begun.

I was the Babe, Joltin' Joe, Ironman Lou,
at the plate and the bases were loaded.
The announcer's voice rang in my head.
"Going, going, gone!" I exploded.

TRAVELING ON

Like Clark Kent effaced by day
in shadow a bland second-string.
But at night "Shazam" I could say,
and the man of steel became King.
Over tall buildings with but single bound,
my mind free to dream in that bed.
No enemy force could come round
and imprison the contents of my head.

Those days now so long in the past.
While some of my dreams did come true
my journey took a much different cast.
Never hit the great home run blast
or was able to fly very fast.

Now in old age I dream other dreams.
Of the things I could do way back then.
As fantastic as Superman they seem.
A time that will not come again.

It's entropy now that I fight.
The urge to lie down and to dream.
I resist the pull with my might.
That I might stay awake and upright.

I am drawn back down into the earth.
That timeless eternity before birth.
The challenge not to run but to walk.
To believe that my life still has worth.

I cannot imagine that room
where there are no tall buildings to leap.
No cheering crowds just a tomb.
The silence of that dreamless last sleep.

Who Else?

(For Karen, Valentine's Day 2015, prior to
my toe amputation)

Who else would want to kiss my toe
and grieve with me its loss?
Who else would want to touch my soul
While trying to be my boss?

Who else's hand is there to hold
when I cannot see ahead?
To keep me warm at night when cold
and walk with me through dread?

Who else would listen to my laments
and praise me, nonetheless?
Argue with all my sentiments
yet believe I'm not a mess?

Who else would think me so worthwhile
As to differ with all I say.
Yet want to wake up with me again
and share another day?

Who else to hold when I am blown?
Who else to be my friend?
Our stormy path ahead unknown
until our fatal end.

Who else could make me love her more
even when she drives me mad?
You My Dear with heart of gold
your presence makes me glad.

Who else could be my Valentine?
No other one will do.
Without you here I'd sadly pine.
The one I want is you.

The Kiss, red cedar

49

Reality

When I look into the starry sky
and believe it's here and now,
it was long ago it all did die,
a fact my mind cannot allow.

The birth of all is what I see.
But does it feel that way?
If it were true how could I be?
Such tricks on self I play.

We believe that dark is nothing.
But it's matter we are told.
The fundamental something.
That together us all does hold.

Our senses tell us to believe.
They inscribe what's really there.
But it's fabric of illusion that they
weave,
and folly to conceive.

And when we look at one another,
what is it that we see?
Adult or child, father, mother,
or reflection of past misery?

Feeding the Birds in Winter

Though the hole should be dug in the land
so the feeder has some place to stand,
as long as fall's warmth lingered round
by those resolutions I would not be bound.

In thrall of illusion I would say
"Another day will come tomorrow."
More important things to do today.
Ever more hours left to borrow.

December snow now o'r spreads the ground.
The birds have nothing to eat.
While soundless snowflakes drift down,
digging's become an impossible feat.

My December is coming as well.
A fact on which I'd best not dwell.
White hair and deepening bony chill.
A stiffness and longing to be still.

Seems sad that I make my mind bend.
To believe death will not take its toll.
And imagine my time will not end.
While deceiving my own starving soul.

Resignation may be here as well.
May be I just don't want to know.
That while I blend into earth's chill,
up above fledgling birds yet will grow.

The body of my next door neighbor was found early in December 2021 by a casual acquaintance whose calls had gone unanswered. Apparently, she had been dead for some time. Margo was one of the few inhabitants of the neighborhood when I moved into the new development 8 months before 9/11. We were never friendly as she was preoccupied with preserving the exact boundaries separating our properties and admonishing me whenever she felt I had trespassed, leaving me with a combination of anger and guilt. She had cement markers put in the ground along with a couple big boulders so as to leave me no doubt. Since learning of her death I have searched the internet in vain for any trace of an obituary, memorial, or even acknowledgement, hoping to learn more about who she was. I have been haunted by her ghost, as lights remain on in her doorway. This effort at poetry is a kind of exorcism.

Margo Crist

Protected the boundaries of her estate
with admonitions and with concrete.
Until her body was found within, too late.
No traces left to explain her fate.

A pop song from her youth did cry
"Give me something to remember you by."
Though she was an archivist of books
she left me naught but haughty looks.

The chambered nautilus on the beach
promises music of French horns within,
til held against my eager ear
echoes nothing but the wail of wind.

Margo Crist.
A name with boundaries crisp
left lights on in the entry
and a question, did she exist?

Mirror, Mirror

I peered into the mirror
and what did I see
but a sour wizened visage
peering balefully at me.

Do we know one another?
Of this face I did ask.
If so, I'm confronted
with an onerous task.

My mother when aged?
That can't be the case.
She surely belongs
to another time and place.

Through her youthful reflection
my self first was faced
in an eager direction
life's cares have replaced.

Next came the fairytales.
Mirror, mirror on the wall
was where one might find
the fairest of them all.

TRAVELING ON

Then on to my youth.
Vainly combing my hair.
In search of a style
that appeared debonair.

Without a mirror held close to my sight
how could I know who was me?
Shackled to such an unfortunate plight
is a most insecure way to be.

Now I'm left with a difficult task.
To search 'neath this strange shocking
mask.
To accept what's before me to see.
And know that most likely it's me.

If I'm repelled by that mask
and reject the reflection I see
and try to go on with life's task
who will go forward with me?

But could this be another misdirection?
Perhaps the flaw in my perception
lies in the eye of its beholder
not in the mirror's stark reflection.

~END~

www.ingramcontent.com/pod-product-compliance
Lightning Source LLC
Chambersburg PA
CBHW051554120626
46551CB00013B/1518